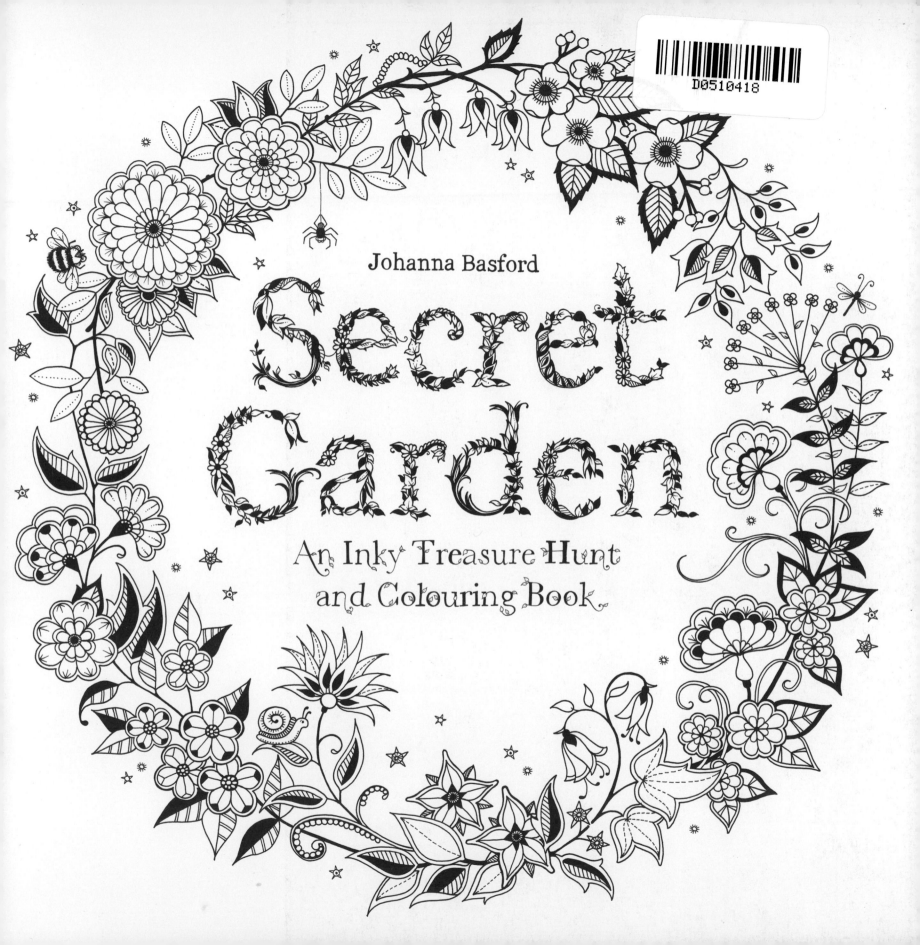

Johanna Basford

Secret Garden

An Inky Treasure Hunt and Colouring Book

LAURENCE KING

Published in 2013 by
Laurence King Publishing Ltd
361-373 City Road
London EC1V 1LR
Tel: +44 20 7841 6900
Fax: +44 20 7841 6910
email: enquiries@laurenceking.com
www.laurenceking.com

Reprinted 2013 (five times), 2014 (six times), 2015 (eighteen times)

A catalogue record for this book is available
from the British Library.

ISBN 13: 978 1 78067 106 2

Design: Jason Ribeiro, Johanna Basford

Printed in The Netherlands

This book belongs to

Hidden inside this book there are...

3 chrysalises

8 spiders

9 dragonflies

14 caterpillars

20 song birds

1 treasure chest

1 hedgehog

1 cat

16 bees

1 squirrel

5 moths

1 padlock

2 hummingbirds

63 beetles

2 frogs

1 shark

4 keys

6 flying beetles

16 ladybirds

5 wasps

13 owls

1 message in a bottle

16 snails

116 butterflies

11 ants

7 slugs

1 peacock

27 fish

3 mice

...Plus a few butterflies and beetles where only a leg or a wing made it onto the page!

At the end of the book is a key that tells exactly what can be found in each picture.

Welcome to my inky world of secret gardens!

Inside this book you'll find a magical black and white wonderland full of fantastical flowers and curious plants.

There are pictures to colour in, mazes to solve, patterns to complete and lots of space for you to add your own inky drawings. Use felt tip pens to add a splash of colour or a black pen with a fine nib to create your own doodles and details.

Peppered throughout the pages you'll spot half hidden creepy crawlies and curious little creatures. Search between the blossoms to find the bumble bees, butterflies and birds that are hidden within.

Use the Secret Garden List to help you keep track of all the things you have found on the inky treasure hunt so far.

Good luck!

Create more caterpillars, chrysalises and butterflies

Add inky
details
to the
flowers...

...and
the
Butterflies

Create
more
Topiary
shapes

Fill the white space with tangles of vines & flowers

Draw here what the padlock is locking away

Fill these pots with plants & Flowers

Draw a swarm of butterflies & blossoms

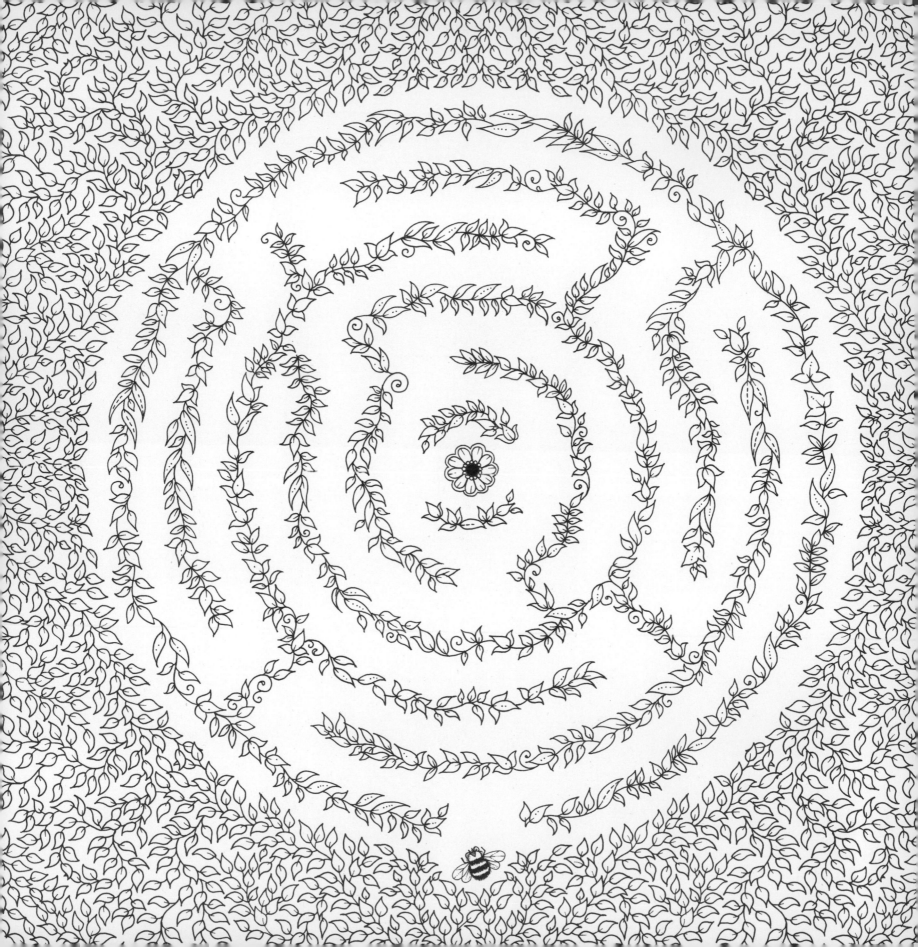

complete the floral pattern

& add lots of inky details

Add
inky
details

surround the sunflower with a swarm of bumble bees

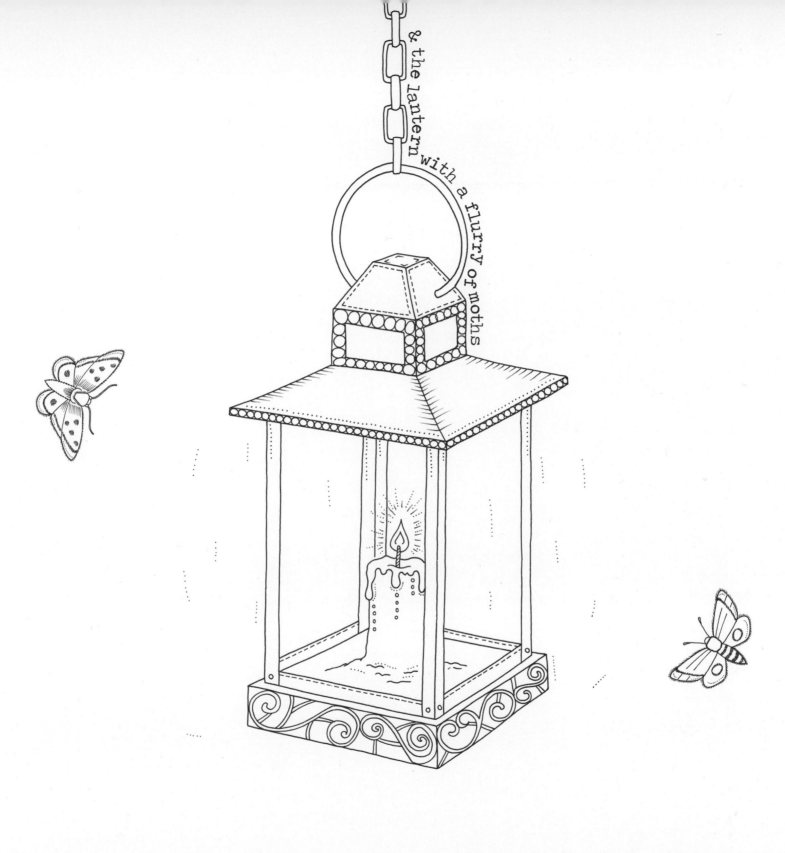

& the lantern with a flurry of moths

Draw a flock of birds perched on the scarecrow

Fill these branches with a chorus of song birds

Create
more
flowering
branches

Continue
the
vine...

...and
fill
with
inky
details

sketch some snails and slugs

Carry
the
key
to the
secret
door

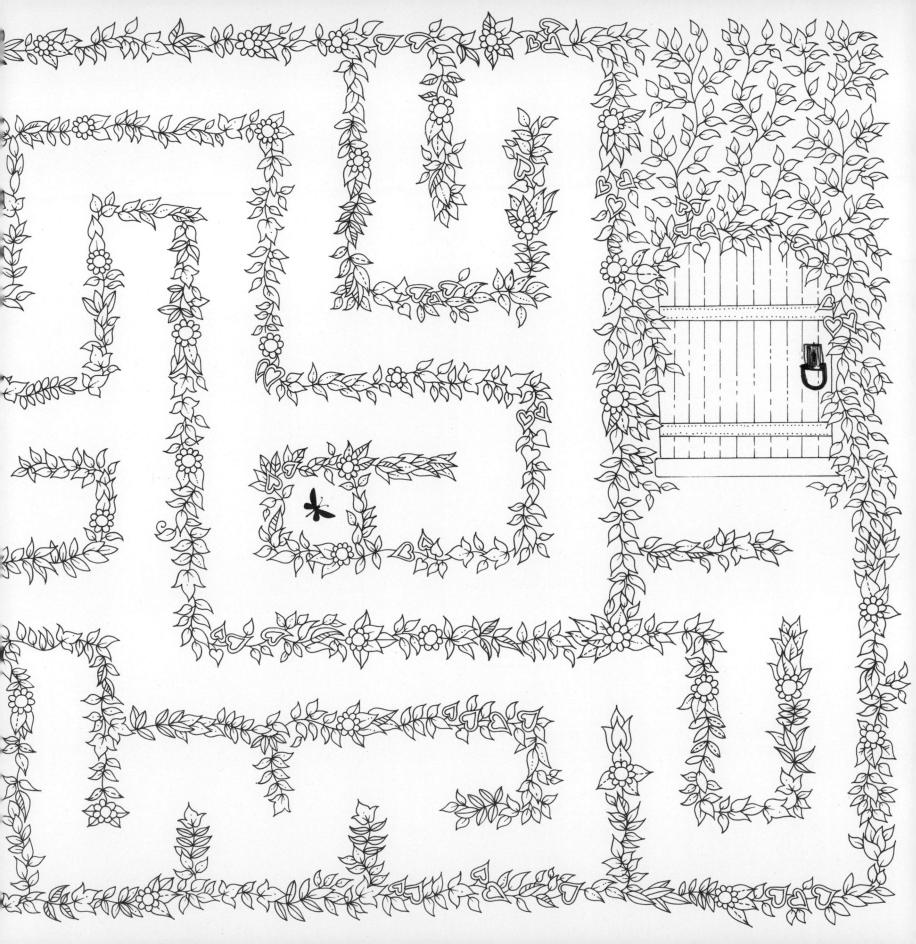

Fill the pond with fish, frogs and lilypads

Grow this garden to fill the page

Draw a swarm of bumble bees

Add pretty inky petals to complete the flower garden

Draw tangles of vines & daisy chains

Fill the white space with tiny leaves & blossoms

Fill the white space with lots of butterflies

Key to the Secret Garden

2 song birds, 1 squirrel, 1 key

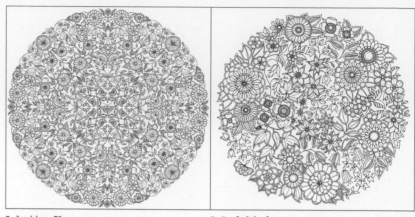

1 butterfly 1 ladybird

1 owl 4 snails

2 owls, 1 bee 6 caterpillars

4 butterflies, 3 caterpillars,
3 chrysalises

7 butterflies

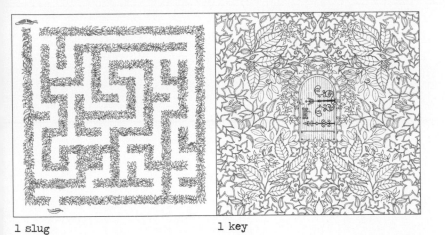

1 slug 1 key

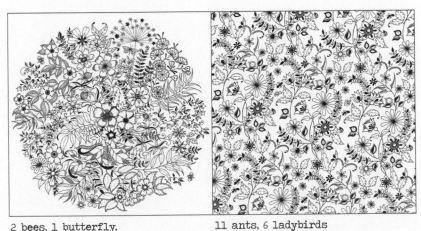

1 mouse

1 key, 1 padlock

2 bees, 1 butterfly,
1 caterpillar 11 ants, 6 ladybirds

4 snails, 2 spiders, 1 caterpillar,
1 mouse, 1 hedgehog

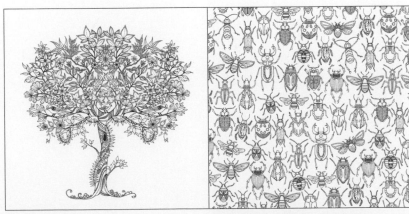

5 song birds 63 beetles, 5 flying beetles,
4 wasps, 2 moths

1 ladybird 1 ladybird

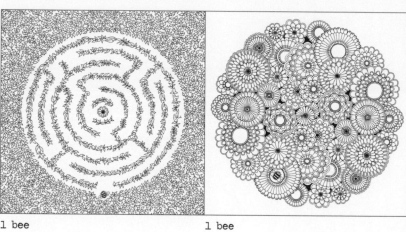

40 butterflies

1 butterfly

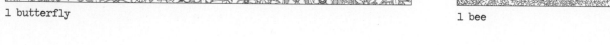

1 bee 1 bee

5 butterflies

2 hummingbirds 1 snail

14 butterflies

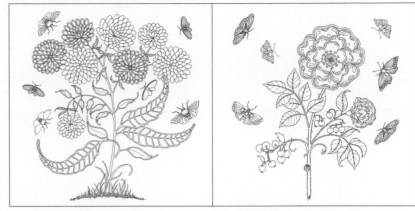

6 butterflies 6 butterflies, 1 ladybird

1 dragonfly 1 spider

2 bees, 2 moths

3 song birds, 2 butterflies,
1 snail

2 spiders 4 butterflies

10 owls

1 butterfly, 1 dragonfly, 1 bee,
1 spider, 1 caterpillar, 1 snail

4 song birds, 1 spider, 1 mouse

3 song birds

1 ladybird

6 butterflies

1 dragonfly

6 slugs, 3 snails

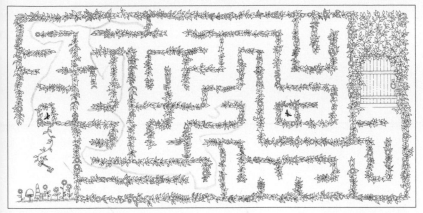

2 butterflies, 1 key

4 butterflies, 1 caterpillar,
1 dragonfly, 1 spider, 1 song bird

2 dragonflies, 1 butterfly,
1 ladybird

1 ladybird

24 fish

2 fish, 2 butterflies,
2 dragonflies, 2 snails, 1 frog,
1 shark, 1 treasure chest,
1 message in a bottle

1 fish, 1 frog

1 moth, 1 wasp,
1 flying beetle

2 bees

4 butterflies, 4 bees, 1 ladybird

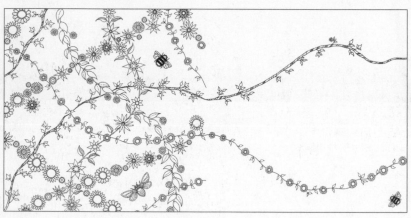

2 bees

2 song birds, 1 cat 1 peacock

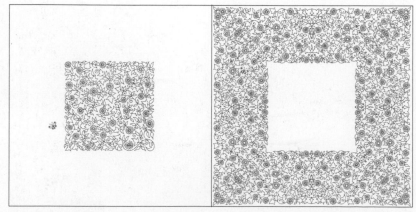

2 butterflies

2 butterflies, 2 ladybirds, 1 butterfly
1 dragonfly, 1 caterpillar